Hear the Pennies Dropping

Peter Strawhan

Hear the Pennies Dropping

Acknowledgements

Huge thanks go to Jane Taylor Robinson, my ever supportive wife – I sure got it right the fourth time, my love! Thanks also to Roger Rees in particular for persuading me that I'm both a poet and a writer and our fellow Sandwriters for their encouragement. Special thanks to Stephen Matthews, who is Ginninderra Press, for starting the ball rolling by publishing my first book of poetry, *Palace of Dreams*.

Hear the Pennies Dropping
ISBN 978 1 76041 069 8
Copyright © Peter Strawhan 2015

First published 2015 by
Ginninderra Press
PO Box 3461 Port Adelaide 5015 Australia
www.ginninderrapress.com.au

Contents

Beyond the Point	9
At Hastings	10
Hastings Continued	11
Parental Guidance	12
On Middleton Beach	14
Reflections	16
Drought	18
Ending the Year	19
Balancing Trick	20
Homecoming	21
Kilcunda	22
Traffic Syndrome	23
Interview Time At the Retreat	24
'Protest In a Violent World'	26
The Way To Frankston	27
Wonthaggi	28
Cowes	29
Every Valley	30
Birthday Celebration	31
A Previous Wife	32
Nitpicker	33
Western Springs – Lakeside	34
Glimmering	35
Derby Castle	36
Bin Day	37
Biology Wins	38
On Larkin	39
Excommunicated	40
Another Ending	41
Whitby: Cook's Town	42

Autumnal Glade	43
Hi Ho! Hi Ho! It's Off To Work We Go	44
Trio	46
A la Metaphysicals	47
Another Fairy Tale	48
No Worries, Mate	49
Reflections On the Redeye	51
Treasures On Exhibition	53
Going Through the Motions	55
Exhibiting Hannaford	56
Crawling Caterpillars	57
What Odds?	58
It's (Whale) Time	59
Droning Not Waving	60
No Bucket List	61
The Corporate Plague	62
It's a Dog's Life	63
White Spray	64
Ah! Memories	65
Cowandilla Primary	66
In Vino Veritas	69
Shearwaters	70
Industrial Mansion	72
Cars Are Us	74
Birth Control	75
Dining At the Club	77
Contemplating Oscar	80
Saturday Delight	82
Morning Glory	83
Black Dog	84
Processing Workers Into Unemployed	85
Sticking It Up the Timorese	86

Wonderful Wagtails	88
The Unhappy Organism	89
Full Moon	90
The Wood Shed	92
Something Passed By	93
To Catch a Wave	95
Ars Longa Vita Brevis	97
Kojunup Coffee, Anyone?	99
19 September 2001	101
On Wrens	102
Hear the Pennies Dropping	103
And Finally	104
The Suicide	105
Tripping Down the Garden Path	108
Spellbound	109
Meditation On Dishwashing	110
On Not Listening	111
The Politics of Envy	113
That's Life	114
At Petaluma	115
Jaqui Hicks Retrospective	116
The Lily Pond	117
No Problem	118
My Friend the Recluse	119
Happy Shopping	121
Post Orstraya Day	124
Dayo, Dayo	125

The rock hits the hard place
The silence shatters
Into screaming shards

Beyond the Point

Etched against the early morning sky
A long white vapour trail
Arrows towards Perth
The wintry sun climbs rapidly
From the eastern horizon
Scattering thin blue ribbons of cloud
Like a starburst: on the beach
Jackie noses into a pile
Of freshly mounded seaweed
That hides the ugly brown stains
Discolouring once pristine sands
A few wetsuited board riders
Ignore cappuccino-coloured breakers
And paddle through toxic-looking sludge
In search of more wholesome water
Further out beyond the point

At Hastings

Civilisation is
A many-splendoured thing
Not only Safeway but Kmart
With toilets
Oh! The relief!

Hastings Continued

Why does that grinning ape
With tatts and half-mast jeans
Keep pushing the thin-faced blonde
With her three small kids
To take a cigarette? Of course
She finally does. Pleased with his victory
He lights her up as they are joined
By her bear-like partner fresh from
The backwoods and in time
To accept his handout the trio
Trail their smoke which winds
Loving tendrils for the kids to enjoy

Parental Guidance

If you won't stay at school
And make the most of your
Opportunity you must have
A trade son what's five years?
Not a bloody eternity
Feels like one
Don't get smart with me
The motorcar is here to stay
So get stuck in and find the way
Cheap labour don't be dumb
You can't expect good money
While you learn the game
Fifteen bob a week?
That's more than I got
When I was your age
So sweep the floor
And get the lunches
Maybe one day
We'll let you fix some punctures
Never mind that bullshit
They teach at trade school
There's only one way
To learn some skills
And that's to work
Not bloody shirk
What do you mean
We should have more equipment?
Use your back and your hands
Not the brain in your head
What, the hammer slipped?

Wipe the tears and swear instead
It's do as I say not do as I do
You've got to learn your place
If you want to stay in the race

On Middleton Beach

Following my shadow
Along the beach this morning
Thinking when I'm gone
So will my shadow presumably
Don't suppose I'll know really
Somehow it seems to matter
Not about me though
Only about that shadow
Moving purposefully ahead
Ah! But now I've turned
It falls dutifully behind
And by so doing
Clears my mind
Each morning I scan
The tideline I'm quite a dab
Hand at picking up all sorts
Of sea-borne detritus
Lately a lovely pair of pink
Swimming goggles and nasty
Fish hooks embedded in plastic
Dummy fish rubber gloves
Golf balls and caps of all varieties
Sunglasses even a black T-shirt
Buried in the sand that once
Washed proved to be my size
I'd love to find a seahorse
Or better still a leafy sea dragon
Others I know have had the
Privilege but not me not yet
Certainly not today have I

Found one of those seemingly
Conceited little creatures
(Like Ogden's swans who can
Only swim whilst sitting down)
Whereas magically horses and
Dragons cruise by standing up
Thereby entitled to be looking smug
Evolution surely has much to answer for

Reflections

Wading through another
Winter of my discontent
Reflecting on the long journey
From a sort of sense
To nonsense not alone
Simply the affliction of age
But was there ever a time
Of sense? Probably not
Reading Bowden on Davis
Makes me regret
That Nixon is dead
Kissinger however is not
Should be crucified
A pair of lying bastards
Poor Cambodia
Khmer Rouge encouraged
To pounce the United States
Will support Cambodia
Till the end of time
Oh, look, they've cut and run
A warning Canberra take heed
You're not listening!
Ask not what America can do
For you! They'll do you anyway
Turning now to Vietnam
Bob said we were invited
(Menzies not Hawke)
Yet another lie
Could any of our so-called
Leaders lie straight in bed?

Obviously not at least today
It's a given we know they're
Lying no more core promises
(Probably all Howard will be
Remembered for!) Why is it so?
The buck no longer stops
Anywhere no care no responsibility

Drought

Nearing the end of our time
We who should not
Fly back
Over the many quilted patches
In their variegated
Drought-shaped hues
Of browns and fawns
Stretching below and beyond
Our flight path then
A convoluted serpent appears
Twisting from north to west
Writhing in agony across
The patchwork remains
Of a desiccated land
Our only lifeline
Now miserable and betrayed

Ending the Year

Wind me up
And point me
Off I go
A good little automaton
But why the tears?

Balancing Trick

Turning the knob
Of the rheostat
I gradually increase
The current flow
Until weightlessness
Overcomes gravity
And I float serenely
Betwixt the constant
Horns of my dilemma

Homecoming

Normal service
Has been resumed
As I retreat from disaster
Yet again this time
A very close call
Right to the brink
Of my particular abyss
Is not too fanciful
The frail edge of sanity
Crumbling away
How good it feels
To be back with you
Basking in our reignited
Love enjoying once more
The sweet happiness
Of your smile

Kilcunda

A sprinkle of seagulls
White dots on distant rocks
Long swelling breakers
Crescendo then plunge
Into foam

Traffic Syndrome

We lemming-like rush blindly on
From one set of lights to the next
At least the lemming need make
No apology his program was preordained
What can be our defence?

Interview Time At the Retreat

Silence – in other words no speech
Except when questioned by our guru
At interview – in a moment or two – shit!
Having missed my allotted time
Sneaking upstairs for a quick
Lie down on the vinyl-covered bunk
As cold as the grave avoiding another
Still vigil with others as they
Dutifully practise surfacing too late
Having no watch with me instead
Waiting now on creaking boards
Facing old wood-panelled walls
Remembering that other corridor
So long ago Creeping Moses we
Called him our headmaster at his pleasure
Back then standing at attention
Palms sweating unbidden in anticipation
As the swishing cane descended
Now sitting palms again moist why?
Not fear of punishment only memories
Of past encounters rising up to trigger
That unseemly response
First learned aged seven perhaps?
Two small returning truants
Again no watch to show the time
Who had watches then?
Only the headmaster hiding behind bushes
Get to my study hold out your hands
Grimy from our play now streaked
With our fear his cane featured

A bent nail at its business end
I cried with pain and peed my pants
My hands were bloodied
So long ago

'Protest In a Violent World'

We gather for another talk fest
Sharing our common strand of concern
Concern at what ails us ails the world
The reality of despair
At humanity's inhumanity
Of America's arrogance and ignorance
Long displayed but now in spades
Post the eleventh of September 2001
As the born again monkey usurps
The driver's seat of the juggernaut
Surrounded by corporate mind sets
Brooking no dissent as they juggle
His lead Achtung! Achtung! Back to
The old Goebbels refrain the swelling
Chorus of hate regains its place
Changing targets for a fairground prize
New demons arise like mandrakes
For another slaughter but our theme
Is non-violence born in Nashville
Where nigrahs once hung from trees
In the sometime land of the free
That battle won for then the cycle broken
Now we begin again
We engage we move on together

The Way To Frankston

Loading her shopping
Into the giant four-wheel drive
Squatting across our bike trail
She flattens herself against
Its sculptured flank as I brush by
We had to park here
Or else we'd bog
That would be a shame
I flung back on the wind

Wonthaggi

The noonday mine whistle
Sounds rheumatically
At seven minutes after the hour
But only the ghosts of miners past
Turn their heads
None of the shoppers heading
In to Woolies or its safer clone
Break their stride or their shuffle
As the case may be
What a civilised town
Why, it even boasts
A McDonalds I see

Cowes

At breakfast
The rodent petrol-head
Tells of bull bars and slaughtered cows
Out on the circuit
The Super V8s
Try to slay each other

Every Valley

An extremely fortunate man
The tenor exalts every valley
On Channel 3 while the cumulus
Plateaus to the horizon
Like whipped cream occasional
Rifts reveal far below the dappled
Green sea Auckland lies behind
With mission accomplished
Sydney closes in ahead
Old friends to meet
Life is good

Birthday Celebration

No rocket's red glare
But you were indeed
'A breath of fresh air'
Exclaiming in surprise
As we met
For that first time
Sipping red wine
Toasting the moment
Sharing poets and poetry
Enjoying synchronicities
Of mind of word
And thought
Then later and still
Love's magic

A Previous Wife

Would it have changed
The course of our history
I wonder? We'll never know
Will we? So what's the point?
Still your urge to confess
The outline of those many
One night stands to your new
Husband cast in the role
Of priest father confessor
The nuns calling to you
Beads clicking through worn fingers
I understand your need
After his betrayal came your revenge
But my gut over rode my heart
I too felt betrayed knowing
We were both far from virginal
Till death us do part
We wept together at the prospect
And soon arranged new lives

Nitpicker

Responding in the usual way
I begin nitpicking
At the knot of our relationship
Determined to destroy
The plus the positive
Not looking at the obvious
Lying within my grasp
Within me
All that unreasoning angst
At my existential void
That is the true nub
Of my discontent

Western Springs – Lakeside

Behind the surfing traffic roar
The green hills lie patiently
Brooding silently in anticipation
While black swan imports wax
Balletic then forage wet lawns
In line astern a coven of ducks
Play Billy Goats Gruff while
Autumn leaves layer at parental feet
Unleashed dogs ignore warning signs
And Pukeko pretend at Swamp Hens
A long way from Gondwanaland

Glimmering

In the motel room
After the opera
As the salt tears
Filled my eyes
Finally you began
To understand
The depths
Of my despair
The place I inhabit

Derby Castle

The old women with faces
Like wrinkled prunes
Set round the table blue rinses
Bobbing half pints of Guinness
Clasped in arthritic hands cigarettes
Jutting from tight-pursed lips
Dissecting the events of their day
Like seagulls picking at a poor
Stranded whale cold bacon
For breakfast and lumpy porridge
And Alice dear such a trial you know
Four operations now and that Bert
You know good for nothing you know
Wonder what's for tea dear?

Bin Day

The squat green sentinels
Poised in waiting
Arrayed in their prescribed
Positions they stretch
Into the middle distance
An occasional gap
Discloses the absent
To possible predators
A remote rumble
Becomes a roaring presence
One by one the guardians
Are plucked skywards
Then ignominiously upended
We who are not privy
To their contents
Can only guess
At what lay within
Neither will those soaring gulls
Share in the feast
Of yesterday's banquet
As once they might

Biology Wins

Just a body or is there more?
The mechanical coupling completed
Lying now uncoupled replete
Senses satisfied glazed over
Sickly as marzipan on a wedding cake
But the mind detached begins teasing
At the old thread like a sleeve unravelling
The nagging doubt emerges naked
Blinking in the face of reality
To be rejected again as incapable of solution
Easier to turn away back against back
Let the familiar process begin again
Until the need for release overcomes logic
The first hesitant overture is returned
And like interest mounts to passion overlaid
The fragile edifice once more erected
Soon collapses as desire is again satisfied

On Larkin

Of course Larkin was right
They fuck you up
Your mum and dad
Ask your own kids
They'll soon tell you
Some do in spades
No – parents, silly
Trouble is
That one put down too many
Then fate takes a hand
Or whatever
Next thing you know
It's too fucking late
All over red rover

Excommunicated

In response to my runaway pen
Your note was effectively a knee
Applied brutally to the groin
Your reaction to my absurd conceit
Echoed the prudishness
Of some mid-Victorian novelist
Or do the little sisters still
Tug occasionally on your strings?
Amongst friends surely warranted
A mild reproof in jesting vein
Not a king-hit to the jugular
Even though you saw
Quasimodo rampant my apology
Would have come running
Excommunication ensured reflection
On the heinous crime instead
Bemusement is my order of the day
Still my honeyed words may
Have papered a hidden trap
You will never know
But lustful fancies like
Speckled backs of ageing hands
May later crowd upon your own
Thoughts in another century

Another Ending

Tears fill the caverns of my eyes
As I look out over the desolate plain
Where all the ruins lie
What little remains of the sparkling domes
The thrusting spires of my lost desires
A rivulet forms carrying more detritus
To the edge of the abyss
The boatman beckons

Whitby: Cook's Town

Through the leadlight squares
Gulls rise and fall
While black crows drift by
Pretending they too are gulls
On the headland Cook stands
Legs astride firm against
The gathering storm clouds
Behind him the whale bones
Describe a different version
Of what is past
In the middle ground
Sideshow alley panders
To the trippers
At the quay side a stumpy tug
In red and white Union Jack
Emblazoned proudly on her flank
Next door a tatty yellow hull
Under the maple leaf the gulls
Masters of their domain
Still dip wheel and soar
Evening sunlight filters
Through the grey I savour
The moment and the scrumpy

Autumnal Glade

On Monday
In our autumnal glade
The soft breeze played
With the dappled leaves
We explored
Each other
With our words
And our caresses
Yet inhibited
By taboos
Not of our making
We passionate paused
On the threshold
Of lovemaking
Today the welcome rain
Strips Monday's bower

Hi Ho! Hi Ho! It's Off To Work We Go

Striding down the hill
The discarded leaves
A riffling carpet
Of autumn brown underfoot
On the opposite side
My counterparts
Have the harder task
But tonight we reverse the process
Nearing the bridge
A cloud of motes dance
In a brief shaft of sunlight
While below
The motionless river
Soils its contoured banks
With an ugly mixture of debris
Perspiring joggers bounce
Along gravelled paths
Or shoulder past occasionally
We meet head on
Causing me a momentary twinge
At their unmasked aggression
Especially en masse
Like a phalanx unarmoured
But bearing down
With heavy thighs and Reeboks
Paid for on Mastercard
A red cape might be handy
For that wobbling cyclist
Picasso would perhaps approve
Or seize another trophy to mount upon

At the end of the path the grass ends
At bitumen and the magic button
Stops the speeding herd
Thus allowing safe negotiation
And work awaits

Trio

We are three
With the silent watcher
In the shadows
Why does he wait?
Silently brooding there
His dark form
Menacing the day
Curdling our joy
We have done no wrong

A la Metaphysicals

Why pine
When times arrow slows
Wrapped in love's veloutinous folds
United soon
We must be
Or else all fails
No gold contained
In tearful memories
Can substitute
Your warm embrace
Not trembling earth
Nor meteor's glare
Can still
The beating of my heart
When you are near

Another Fairy Tale

I weave for you
The cloak of my desire
Made up of all my
Longing of all my loving
Threaded through with
New ways of seeing
New ways of being
That you continue
To show me
As you open my eyes
To new delights
The colour of a flower
The curve of a leaf
All contained in the touch
Of your hand
The bright treasure
Of your smile

No Worries, Mate

On the level playing field
At this point in time
The reality is
There isn't a hurdler
Or pole vaulter in sight*
The bottom line is
Set to be
No worries y'know
Caught as we are
Between a rock
And a hard place
The only window
Of opportunity
For the first cab
Off the rank
Is the choice y'know
Between a pine box
Laid tenderly to rest
In the Bay of Biscay
Or more hygienically
The neater final solution
Y'know is set to be
A small mound of
Whitish ash carefully
Contained in an earthenware
Pot to stand by the Xmas
Cards on their mantelpiece
Or sprinkled on the roses
Perhaps next time y'know
At the end of the day

As a grasshopper
Or a field mouse
Quite frankly things like
Without coke y'know
May well go better
Have a nice day
No worries

* See Jack Hibberd, *A Stretch of the Imagination*

Reflections On the Redeye

A six-pack of hosties
(Er, sorry, flight attendants)
Whinnies past
Moulded on the same production line
From different crucibles
Absurd Akubras (to keep the sun off
On those long flights) shielding
Tight make up from the fluoros' glare
Towing pigskin overnighters
Between fresh comfort stations
Their haute posture
Signalling disdain for
Small bearded ancients
Who have no part to play
In their cosmic scheme of things
Six abreast we jam obediently
Into our allocated slots
After the awkward antagonism
Of shedding and stowing ends
Buried in my copy of *The Guardian*
While the mandatory safety lesson
Runs its well intended course
I draw the aisle crow
Both coming and going
Suffering accordingly for my sins
From the trolley's hard edge
Which echoes an autoclave
It's sterilised load the high point
Of our journeying though the mini
Of Mildara red (five dollars please)

Helps remove that hint of formaldehyde
I dared to touch the passing sleeve
With my small request though
Those business suits opposite
Had no such need the seat belts'
Light draws the ritual passage
To its close as we are thanked
Fulsomely for our patronage
Who was it said 'Make my day'?

Treasures On Exhibition

Some kneel in awe-full contemplation
Before these selective extracts
From the records of past governments
Of this state 'Great place once'
The white haired matriarch mutters
Clutching handbag to cardigan exits
Like a ship of the line looking straight ahead
Some how avoiding
The entrance to the Men's
'My ancestors came out on the *Tam O'Shanter*
Well before the *Buffalo*
Never rates a mention!
I've always wondered why?'
This from the dapper
Still sprightly gent
Trimmed moustache positively
Bristling with self-righteousness
While tight bummed jeans
With tits and tats pads disdainfully by
Past our silent exhibits
Still – tank tops and grubby joggers
Make a change from twin sets and pearls
This lot too the new great unwashed peer briefly
And as quickly disappear
Yes when you get to the escalator turn right
Then head through toys but
Try not to linger at the train
The sign says TOILETS and if
You look carefully exhibition hall
A significant conjunction

Turn left through the double doors can't miss
The loos do a better trade than us
Though we get a share
Of the passing parade
She on high commands
'Don't forget to push the button
On the little counter'
Click! Click! Must have our stats
To justify the exercise
Look a shyly poking head hovers
Only tentatively into view

And as rapidly withdraws
Before the frightened feet step
Cautiously across our threshold
Others stride boldly through
With bright and lavish 'Good mornings'
We their paid servants turn and nod
Maybe even stretch a smile
Some query plaintively 'Do we have to pay?'
Complete with expectant pause
Reluctant fingers hovering
Over purse catch thinking no doubt
Of the dwindling housekeeping
To be fair slowly our week grinds on
To its welcome end
Other chosen do the packing up
And careful returning
Lines of demarcation thankfully maintained

Going Through the Motions

This is the way
I've lived my life
Going through the motions
Never plunging headlong
In to the maelstrom
Always relying
On a back-up position
Making sure to wear
Clean underpants
In case of accident
Of vital import
My dear
And beware
What the neighbours
Might think

Exhibiting Hannaford

Tending the Hannaford
Our blockbuster for the year
I muse inevitably on fickle fate
What did it take I wonder
Guts self-belief a mighty ego?
Secure in self-knowledge
No art school needed
To begin a brace of fortuitous
Mentors came in handy
Hans for red and other gums
Ivor captured the persona
In portrait with horse
And other flesh close by
Riverton farm no doubt
Reinforced the quiet bucolic
Though none of this explains
Cartooning which couldn't last
Given the *Advertiser*'s conjunction
With all things conservative no
The man is no dwarf artist
In a land of pygmies he stands
Tall having demonstrated more
Than mere talent

Crawling Caterpillars

A crawling caterpillar convoy
Of cars heading slowly along
Dutifully following its dawdling leader
Driving at his or hers own happy pace
Maybe an instinctive threshold
Might lose control at 81 and
Any way mother knows best
Even as passenger
Or better still driving
From the back seat
A fine Sunday tradition
Besides what's the rush?
100 in the old money
Is still only what? – 60 or so
Hardly the speed of light
And we are in Orstraya
And it's only the 21st century
Hopefully the last but
Don't aim to be around
When the petrol taps turn dry

What Odds?

This is surely one for Ripley
Remember *Believe It Or Not*?
Showing my age now
Two mornings back on
The familiar beach
Walking along the tidelines offerings
One small crab attracted
My attention feebly waving
The right hand of its two long
Front legs each completely
Disproportionate to a tiny pink body
Obviously in distress: picking it up
I hastened down to a quiet rivulet
Hoping the incoming tide might provide
The kiss of life
This morning strolling a fresh line
Of sea grass balls in their thousands
Brain-shaped fronds countless cockles
All bound loosely in seaweed
Sighting a lady's pink riding crop
Triggered a fleeting memory
Of that singular long-armed crab
In extremis within minutes
It lay again at my feet
Now minus the sinister arm
Otherwise intact but the pink
Already fading fast to grey
What odds that it should again
Appear what odds?

It's (Whale) Time

Spotted the first whale
Of this new season today
Earlier a fair distance off
The beach probably as far
Away as Labor's chances
In the looming election
The seemingly no longer mad
Latham now makes sane commentary
Unlike Murdoch's tame nasties
Who glibly form the specious flow
Spraying forth unabated
From the Libs' lycra-clad bully boy
Look at me I love you all
Yeay down to the last boat person
Gay or Aboriginal even women
We who were born to rule
Only my side can handle money
Balance the books simple really
Like any householder you don't
Spend more than you earn
Well running a country's just the same
Stands to reason doesn't it and
This time we'll privatise the bloody ABC
Along with anything we missed last time

Droning Not Waving

Obama's quick change in the phone box
Sees him leave behind the mild-mannered
Professor of law and emerge not in the
Expected guise as the latest American
Superhero instead shock horror dons his
Retarded predecessor's apeman outfit
The better to administer the lore of the jungle
By fondling the levers of drone control
'Scuse me Mr President how many enemies
Of your state have you obliterated today?
How many US citizens are on your list
To hit and how many innocents have you
Added to the long and ever growing total
You call 'collateral damage': Sleeping well
Are we Mr President? So much for your
Hollow promises strange how the oval office
Shapes each of its temporary residents and
What about the spying how goes the prying?
Even the surviving Stasi must envy
Your machinery of surveillance that electronic
Masterwork but what price freedom and
What price democracy? The founding fathers
Of your hallowed federation lie uneasy
In their graves whispering to each other
At the overturning of their vision
As the forgotten in Guantanamo rot
While their thick-necked guards grow
Ever fatter: another of your promises broken

No Bucket List

No it's not yet over
More battles yet to win
Other mountains waiting
To be climbed further
Brain surgeries to be performed
Another series of grand prix
Yet to win while the magic isle
Still beckons a challenging
Lap record yet to best
Maybe an Archibald or two
I'll win maybe that life-sized
Bronze to pour what is that land
On the far horizon? Ah!
Machu Picchu perhaps next year
How many books on shelves
Unread? Keep all your bucket lists
And stand well back as I light
The blue touchpaper for another
Blast off: But with the bang
My universe failed to expand
Soon like Icarus my own ephemeral
Wings were in tatters and once more
I crashed back to earth
Where only battered windmills
Stood silently in rebuke

The Corporate Plague

A plague on all your corporate
Houses and all of your meaningless
Mission statements and your smart
Phones with their touch me please
Touch me here screens oh! so finger
Licking good! And about as nourishing
May you all melt down in the manner
Of your oh! so great financial system
Designed to fill that empty void
That passeth all understanding yes
Greed my corporate friends keep up
That good work screwing the weak
The malnourished poor with all those
Wondrous projects that continue
To pollute and blacken and besmirch
In the hallowed name of development

It's a Dog's Life

Think I'll just lie down for a bit
Here on my bed in the corner
Of the deck might make my way
Down those steps in a while prefer
Lying under there when it gets a touch
Too warm up top need to catch my breath
Rest these ancient bones the hip hole I dug in
The last year or so helps me rest pretty comfy really
Been some time since brekky and no walk today as yet
Oh! Hello! He's decided to acknowledge me
Just appeared with one of those tough old biscuits
Yes mate I'm still among the living they're real hard
Tack takes him all his strength to break them into four
Pieces on the table's edge don't really appeal these days
Teeth aren't what they used to be still
Shouldn't complain too much at least I'm
Getting fed outside of course not allowed inside
Since I started dribbling pee on their shiny ersatz
Timber floor that odd couple from down the road
Always slide open the side door make a fuss
Even let me in for more pats but madam and him
The alpha male say NO! Out she goes not my fault
I'm so old ninety something they reckon in their
Terms so why shouldn't I still come in mans'
Best friend can't stay a cuddly pup for ever
Wait till they get to my age they'll see 'course
He's still a bit pissed off with me can I help it
If he trod in the little surprise I let drop on
The gravel by the rainwater tank this morning
Early trap for the unwary needs to open his eyes
Doesn't he!

White Spray

The fiercely gusting winds
Pluck white spray from atop
The long line of cresting
Breakers reminder of yesterday's
Recumbent whales letting off
Their brief clouds of steam
Proving to those in any doubt
That they are not mere fish
Destined to feed the hungry
Multitudes but once walked
The land as our own developing
Kind swam in primeval seas
Mere seconds past in earth's time

Ah! Memories

The old Overland Whippet
Had a gear lever knob
That looked as if it was
Made of frozen milk toffee
My sister perched on our
Father's lap as he drove
Towards Lipsett Terrace
And he let her take the wheel
Aw gee can't I have a go?
Leaning across on the horsehair
Stuffed seat I succeeded only
In arousing the quick flare
Of his anger as the car veered
Right then left as I over-corrected
Leave it alone will you! He cried
You're hopeless you've got no idea
I retreated snail-like into the safety
Of my familiar shell smarting
The hurt lingering over the years

Cowandilla Primary

Please sir – as I put my hand up
Bob Minear's an uncle. Mister Waters
Was good as teachers go especially
In the 1940s but even he couldn't resist
Slamming shut the door of understanding
In my eager face as I stood anxious
To gain his acceptance the rest of grades
Six and seven laughed in raucous delight
As he paraded my naivete before them
Sit down Strawhan how I hated that name
Rhymes with prawn 'seeder prawn'
They sometimes chanted at recess time
With the asphalt hot underfoot I was nonplussed
To me with only one younger sister it was
Beyond belief Bob Minear an uncle how could
This possibly be? Down the years it sometimes
Surfaced to join the throng of long remembered
Put downs in grades three and four Mr Jones
Had yellow skin and bet on race horses
We were made to listen. School of the Air
Became race of the day from the wireless
Sitting on the mantelpiece over the open
But empty fireplace in our cold classroom
I was disgusted. How dare he inflict this shame
On us we were there to learn of higher things
Or so I priggishly believed. How could this be?
If your leg shook with nerves (like Dad's)
He – Jonesy – threatened to tie the offending
Member to the cast-iron desk leg for me
Ever obedient the mere threat was enough

My palsy-like quivering soon stopped
Others who did not perhaps could not exercise
The requisite self-control paid the price
As Jonesy grabbed his length of binders' twine
And swiftly bound their jiggling leg to stillness
They dared not touch until the bell knelled
The only bright star in our dreary firmament
Of long days suffered thanks to the jaundiced
Jones was the prospect of grade five under
The near-deified Mister Mader he whose pupils
Without it seemed exception adored him
Our expectation of release from the clutches of
The yellowed Jones were dashed when news
Spread that Mader stood to be transferred
To another luckier school desperate measures
Were called for I composed a petition a precocious
Missive to the unknown authorities of the education
Department and all the kids when called upon
Signed their names please don't transfer our Mister
Mader not knowing the protocol my scrawl was last
So the sweet innocent was it Shirley Burns? Whose
Name headed the list was summoned to the headmaster's
Sanctum within a few days in tears she pointed
To my name old Nancarrow bristled like a terrier
Under the inspector's accusing eye he thundered
At my temerity in questioning the judgement
Of the gods never, never dare to do such a heinous
Thing again no sir, no sir, three bags full sir
I will hide my shame like a good little boy
In my tight little shell for ever and ever amen

Though I hope Mister yellow Jones was burned
In Hell 'cos he smoked too I'd forgotten that
The fag end also yellow drooping from the corner
Of his thin-lipped mouth as he whacked his heavy
Wooden ruler on the nearest desk just to see us jump

In Vino Veritas

After sex has lost
Its enchantment
When the bedroom
No longer beckons
When the glimpse
Of pink nipple
Briefly exposed
No longer excites
Even the imagination
When nubile maidens
Swaying past with smooth
Round buttocks signalling
Fuck me! Fuck me!
Fail to blip the needle
Of desire and only oblivion
Beckons there still remains
One consolation prize
That needs must be seized
And raised to quivering lips
As the gods long ago decreed
Ah! Bacchus, Bacchus
Let thy rich red juice
Forever run free

Shearwaters

A long line of dead
And dying mutton birds
Dot the coastal sands
Some still alive lie
Quietly pointed seaward
Seemingly only with sufficient
Energy left with which to make
The transition from barely alive
To barely dead yet always there
Must be a non-conformist
As the one who's left leg jerks
Backwards and then forwards
Incessantly so that the webbed
Foot has scribed a narrow channel
In the wet sand beneath the dark
Travel-stained wing I pause
And briefly consider picking up
The small feathered bundle
Too late for rescue but cannot
Bring myself to end its suffering
By breaking its neck the way we
As school boys once despatched
Rabbits caught in our cruel steel-
Jawed traps without a second's pause
In the great scheme of things why ever
Do the shearwaters aka mutton birds
In their squadrons make this annual
Pilgrimage from stormy Bass Strait
Streaming northwards across those
Vast distances to the rising sun

But then wheeling and turning
Guided by some mystic means
Implanted countless generations
Ago now triggered in time to direct
Their path homewards towards
The great southland where weary
Survivors conceive and nest and
Bring forth another generation

Industrial Mansion

Against the grey morning sky
The tall crane boom appeared
Almost magically an ominous portent
For the red brick tile roofed escapee
From suburbia huddled anxiously
On the corner block next door with its
Oh! So desirable ocean views
Parked nearby a semi-trailer groans
Under the weight of huge cast-concrete slabs
Tradies in now obligatory 'safety' jackets
Of yellow and red plastic with hard hats
Perched precariously on weathered skulls
Swarmed while riggers rigged lines
Soon the first section of this mad hatter's
Industrial-like edifice rose effortlessly
Then slotted down into its allotted space
I shook my head in disbelief and walked
Down to the familiar beach trying
Not to visualise the end product
Of some computer nerd architect's
Fevered brow this was to be a family home?
Next morning my worst fears were realised
Another windowless slab-sided Woolworths
Look-a-like monstrosity reared in total ugliness
Dwarfing its neighbour and all the rest
Stretching in despair along the beachfront
Seeming to sag as each beheld the stark reality
Of the behemoth portending unwanted change
To their cosy weekend only enclave
Why don't they do something about it?

Uneasy murmurs waft on the sea-tanged breeze
It's not fair! Surely they could have stopped
This kind of development?
Ah! Sorry my friends but that is the magic word
Beloved of all small-minded mutants beavering
Away in the various tiers of government
'Development'
What a singular cachet it has what doors
It opens and with such remarkable ease
How mates reach out to mates and what favours
Are called in all to satisfy some clown's towering ego
'Development'
Savour the ease with which it rolls
Off the tongue but whatever you do
Don't think about and certainly
Don't dwell on what it always costs
The mundane little people and further
Punishes the (Dirty Word) environment
Our derivative culture is of course unblemished

Cars Are Us

I observe the older of the two arrive first each morning
He backs and fills the big Ford near the fireplug
Best selling 'Family Car' in Oz we are told. Dear God!
He displays a not unexpected lack of skill
Eventually satisfied with the positioning of the shining
Apple of his eye he switches off and waits
The second one hoves into view within five minutes or so
Speeding around the square he flashes past
Sizing up the situation brakes reverses
Manoeuvres his battered Datsun into the indicated space
Behind the Ford his driving is brutishly efficient
But the scarred flanks of his car signal a warning
The Ford's driver gets out walks across the road
To the park and stands waiting his shoulders
Smoothly hunched under the once trendy sports coat
He appears not to notice the morning air's wintry bite
The beer gut is evidence of suitable insulation
His paunch is matched by the Datsun's driver
Who although younger is as well endowed
They nod and mumble greetings to each other
While ritually lighting the inevitable cigarettes
Surrounded by a haze of blue smoke
They drift off to begin their working day
I watch them go then refocus my camera
On the intriguing bole of the ancient pepper tree
Rejoicing in my good fortune

Birth Control

Was it lust or was it love?
Doesn't matter really
The end results the same
Babies little ones look
His father's nose mother's eyes
How cute there's more
Just as well we never know
What nature has in store
Pigeon pairs proliferate
Twins and triplets exacerbate
Why stop at four or maybe five
Going for the record an Aunt
Had ten cricket team anyone?
Go on make a quid populate
Or perish remember yellow at your peril
Endowments king now that's the thing
But word of warning to the wise once
That head first appears pushed with mother's
Straining paining energy it's now too late
No going back like a joey clawing at the pouch
Baby child teen Goth or obscene lout Sex drugs
Rock and roll will out learners learning
Mates dead or burning Cars crashing police
Emergency maybe lucky odd jobs don't last
Fast food service perhaps university. Phew!
Adults at last but wait on fate like Aunty Kate
There's no escape good old Mum and Dad
Three or four-bedroom brick-veneer going spare
Yes dear still your room jobless girlfriend who?
Pregnant wants to have it! I just don't know

Dad! Please keep it low Christ! Give it a fucking go
Once you've had them they're yours for life
Think everlasting strife unless by chance
Grandparenting's your own wanton vice

Dining At the Club

We'd come up from the south
To visit her mother and the new husband
A touch incestuous really nothing like a bit
Of recycling Lofty hanging loose since
Her sister divorced him force of gravity
Probably not a bad bloke really
Vonny soon vacuumed him up
Into her orbit didn't even need house-training
Nothing like keeping it in the family
I suppose her daughter had caught
My ever roving eye a year or two before
More's the pity as it was turning out
Never marry on the rebound my boy
Too late to heed sound advice yet again
Not clever anyway here we were in
Whatever town it was depending on
Which side of the river same, same
Only different as the market girls say
In Vietnam mind you a leagues club
Is a leagues club seems to me basically
Your Aussie awful writ large
On the way in we selected from the chalkboard
Arranged strategically so we must
Block the doorway by the cash register
Once over the usual dilemma
Of selection (fortunately no desserts required)
Payment made my treat to the unsmiling
Attendant not amused by our minor key levity
On the subject of chicken cacciatore
And value for money at least we'd complied

With the dress code no tank tops colours or thongs
(No dear not the Clinton kind – flip-flops)
Thus gaining entry to the delights within
Along with the rest of the great Saturday
Night unwashed somewhat subdued
We arranged ourselves appropriately
Elbows on poorly wiped laminex
While Lofty braved the distant bar
Looking for Riesling by the glass to start
With no joy bottle service only Friday
Or Saturday nights
Please be seated and thirstily await
The coming of the drink waiter
The faces at the next table were
Profiles by Durer or Bosch
Except for the Asian who was clearly
A ring in still they went well with the décor
Sydney leagues club ocker out of kitsch
With a dash of 50s Hollywood
The drinks person was tricked out
In a tux but sounded punch drunk
Looked glazed-eyed for one so young
On speed maybe our parched throats
Now demanded wine in a bottle
Quickly pretty please 'Sorry mate
I don't serve the champagne (This seriously!)
Youse can have wine by the glass.'
'Two whites then and two reds please.'
He nodded and headed off for a time
Returned empty-handed 'Sorry mate

No red.' We contained our disbelief
And our mirth somebody had their wires
Well and truly crossed or were we simply
Too far north? Mafeking was at last
Relieved with the arrival of our meal
While the ever-patient Lofty made
His stalwart way towards that far distant
Oasis in this place of drought

Contemplating Oscar

Dear Oscar you will recall
Summed it up in his usual
Inimitable fashion just three
Words suffice plucked from
The body of his commentary
Ludicrous momentary prohibitive
No need I'm sure to fill the
In-betweens who knows what Bosie
Thought for poor Oscar the cost
Of his wayward escape from marital
Bliss proved worse than prohibitive
Dwelling on such matters of mind
And body as one does thoughts of
Loves past form like protozoa and
Shape themselves inevitably into
Remembered forms conjuring first
Moments with that other seen naked
For the first time no longer concealed
Breasts revealed bared touched and
Fondled licked and sucked lips bruised
By a myriad of kisses then parted for
Intrusive tongues Ah! Bliss then further
Exploration tracing downward smooth
Inner thighs softly caressed while pausing
For contemplation of that greatest mystery
The veiled portal sought for all eternity
Entry eased by sweet moisture ultimate
Ambrosia body fluids exchanged intermingled
Perhaps a new life approved or as easily
Denied then soon when novelty has

Flown replaced by repetition and worse
Passionless habit with cold evaluation
Replacing initial ardour thoughts of new
Conquests build and like waves crescendo
Until a new encounter again sets the scene
The board wiped clean at first a fresh sweet
Face then soon enough the body follows
To be sipped and savoured and revered
Perhaps to be remembered by an old lover
Writing lines of love and lust

Saturday Delight

Our usual Saturday morning
Beach walk with another couple
Oldish friends happy with each other
And it seems with us afterwards
Repairing for coffee that necessary
Recharge re-boosting our caffeine
Levels and vital functions four
Young women variously obese
Occupy the next table presumably
Friends at least acquaintances
Communicating not across the
Common divide not eyeballing
Each other not speaking to each
Other instead fingers flicking
Flying texting messages thoughts
Non-thoughts all the momentous
Trivia of their cosy existence
To another set another circle
Similarly engaged similarly disposed
On and outwards engulfing reality
Demeaning and diminishing all of us

Morning Glory

Three magpies chorusing
Atop a Stobie pole
Pouring out their liquid gold
Against the cool grey sky
Of early morning
Reviving my flagging spirits
After yesterday's stultifying heat

Black Dog

Large ugly and unattended
The black dog bounded over
Rocks to a clear patch of sand
And deposited a mighty crap
Relieved at leaving this noxious
Load behind for beach lovers to
Enjoy it swiftly disappeared
This I observed from a safe distance
Wondering what it is that attracts
So many seemingly sane people
To own such beasts no dog lover
I confess self-evidently in my
Eyes so undesirable so unattractive
Surely confirmation of my belief
Lies in their adoption as the symbol
The universal appellation for the ever
Rising scourge we call depression
A defecating black dog certainly
Does it for me please pass the razor blade
Or that box of pills on the bedside table

Processing Workers Into Unemployed

The Lycra clad bully boy dares to denigrate process workers
Who he alleges bludge on cushions of largesse provided
By corporate giant Amatil purveyors of doped sugar water
To the mindless millions a typical multinational concerned
Only with their bottom line their shareholders and their management
Teams where CEOs struggle along on stratospheric salaries
Reputedly 300 times the menial workers norm at last count
They like Abbott and his cohort of like-minded parasites
Are far removed from the dreary reality of shop floor life
In spite of which and all evidence to the contrary they always
Blame the workers and the unions when profits fall as the dollar climbs
The shareholders moan and the banks tighten get out the whips
Sack the lazy drones come on come on work work harder longer
But wait who has the say who plays with the markets who pushes the
Buttons arranges the floats the takeovers the write offs and all of
Those jokes then skims off the proceeds to bottomless accounts
Not the worker the wage slave they can only wait for the axe to fall
And lest we forget its goodbye to Alcoa how many dollars did it take
How many pollies did you need to win before you deigned to honour
Our humble kowtowing shores now looking at the balance sheet
How much have you cost the taxpayer with all those lovely subsidies
And your outrageous and profligate demands for cheap power how
Much sacred land have your bulldozers destroyed and how many first
Nation lives corrupted with money and booze that mammoth flagpole
Standing like Gulliver's tribute to our Lilliputian capital will remind
Those who care to think once upon a time the honourable Paul Keating
World's greatest treasurer (ask him) declaimed that this is as good as it
Gets he was right of course now all the flying armadas are winging
Home to roost

Sticking It Up the Timorese

In Vietnam we had the ugly American
Earlier a Labor prime minister gave us
ASIO learning from our newest imperial
Role model they who we now obey other
Acronyms for secret organisations soon
Proliferated while we surrendered our
Precarious nationhood providing secure
Hidden places in the so-called national
Interest more accurately to support the
Ever-growing hegemony of our great and
Noble ally while we the people slumbered
On East Timor brought to light the ugly
Australian although his gestation began
A bit earlier in poor shattered Iraq remember
The wheat board scandal any one? What?
Our leaders are into bribery and corruption?
Never! Well hardly ever simpering Downer
He of the fish net stockings failed liberal
Leader escaped even the mildest censure
But happily played his role when we honest
Word of honour Aussies shafted the still
Shell-shocked Timorese to take the lion's
Share of wealth the gas and oil from under
Their high seas using electronic eaves dropping
By stealth fast forward to today and our spooks
Raid and plunder evidence that supports
The Timorese in a London court enough
Time to wake up all of you out there time
To enter the real world at long last forget
The hallowed past the mythical ANZAC blast

Pull your heads from the complacent sands
Where Howard lulled you to lie comfortable
And relaxed while he basked in the sunshine
Of mad W's smile stand on the parapet and
Survey this nation's mounting decay don't
Let the spineless mob who lead us have
Their wrongful way instead support the
Just cause of the long suffering Timorese.

Wonderful Wagtails

A busy band of Willie Wagtails
All harum-scarum
Pitching in scrum together
Brothers sisters uncles aunts
Mums and dads cousins too no doubt
Joining their happy revels
Something not within my ken
Attracted them to that particular
Hardy sea side shrub perhaps insects
Hiding in its shade or just simply
Their morning playground
They dive in and out
Darting flirting dancing on the sand
Tails flicking endlessly
Coquettish fans of sheer delight
All displaying their lifelong skills
Though only playing
But don't be fooled
They'll take on a Magpie anytime
And see them off nipping at their
Tail feathers like a cattle dog
Shifting cows or a fighter pilot
Chasing a Fokker with
Machine guns chattering
Willies will always fight and win

The Unhappy Organism

The organism is unhappy decidedly
Unhappy something has tipped the scales
Disturbed the balance a fly in the ointment
Triggering unwanted change and not for
The better it would seem ominous portent
Vomiting up the usual healthy breakfast
A new experience surely not morning
Sickness? Just a passing whim a not so
Funny joke an attempt at amusement
To help combat the pain worse in the night
The early morning lying there thinking
What to do trying not to panic trying
For control not succeeding maybe the arms
Will burst or the head can't seem to place
It where the neck won't scream now the hands
Chime in with fingers numbing down down
The chain of bones chasing round the pelvic girdle
Hip bone connected to the thigh bones all
Getting in on the act the new incessant chorus
Old man Old man your time has come
Harken to the tolling bell pen make haste

Full Moon

Went out and bayed
At the moon last night
Been thinking about doing it
For a while now Why ever not?
With the inmates well and truly
Running the asylum what else
Is a man to do?
Climbed out of the old cot
About three a.m. missus snoring
Away in slumberland dressed in the dark
Of course outside plenty of light
From that big bright full moon
Bombers' Moon they used to say
Picked me way down the back
Climbed through the fence
Shit! Bit of a rip in the old jeans
Fucking barbed wire never mind
Away up the hill through the scrub
Bit of a clearing at the top been awhile
Good view down the coast lot of sea
Lot of nothing out there bit like the rest
Of the country really
Anyway did a bit of a jig sort of a warm up
Like them ballet dancers I suppose
Took a few deep breaths hands on hips
Stuck me head up in the cool night air
Bit of a breeze felt good real good
Then let her rip AWOOOOOOOOOO!
AWOOOOOOOOOO! AWOOOOOOOOOO!
Stopped to listen nothing not a bloody sausage

Only something ran off away from me
Into the bushes then some way off a bloody crow
Let out a cark that died in its throat
Otherwise All Quiet On the Western Front
Not a twitter from the north south or east either
So after a bit of a pause I built up another
Head of steam and let fly again AWOOOOOOOOOO!
AWOOOOOOOOOO! AWOOOOOOOOOO!
Back down the hill the world slumbered on
I'd a thought someone down there in the dark
Must have heard might have stirred might have noticed

Nothing well bugger me I thought
Man might as well be dead
Still there's always the next
Full moon maybe I'll make a megaphone
You know like the barkers at the show
Used to have Roll up! Roll up!
Anything off the top shelf four rings
For sixpence come on have a go
Or better still find one of them
Loud hailers maybe at bloody
Garage sale now there's a clue!
Man's got to do something

The Wood Shed

Just imagine
All those years
Frightened
Of an old wood shed
Someone finally
Prised open
The cobwebbed door
Rusted steel hinges
Screamed a protest
Black void within
Parted before inquisitive
Hand-held flickering candle
Nothing nasty in there
After all those many years
Just a scattered pile
Dust shrouded Mallee roots
Nothing nasty
In this wood shed

(With due deference to Stark Adder farm)

Something Passed By

Something passed by
My mind's eye
As I mainly dozed
I almost had it
In my grasp
Just then
In a millisecond
Unbidden
Somewhere a synapse
Touched another
Connection
Perhaps
Just long enough
To register
Somewhere
In the cortex
The cerebellum maybe
Not a starburst
From Callas
Or a tiny tone
From Dupre's
Bow string
No
Too brief by far
Not repeated
A flicker of light
Will of the wisp
Nothing to conjure with
Brief touch
Lover's fingertip

Try and find
Try harder
Agonise!
No! Stop! Stop!
Wrong pathway
There
Dew glistens on a leaf
The leaf falls
No: wait

There, a flavour
It was a flavour
Vapour's zest
On the tongue
From childhood
Too brief even
For saliva to flow
Too brief
Even to imagine

To Catch a Wave

A trio of brawny surfers balancing boards
Clambered awkwardly over the guardian rocks
Anxious to catch a wave
Nearby a trim young blonde limbered up
On the welcoming sand
Then satisfied with her preparation waded out
Steadying the long board
With the ease of familiarity
Then burst from the foam
Like a leaping dolphin
To lie easily on board
and paddled seaward
Black wetsuit glistening
Towards the waiting line of expectant breakers
Nearby the nanny state
Ever-intrusive ever-watchful
Displayed an ugly patronising sign
Warning of possibilities
No one headed no one needed
And of course penalties apply for those in breach
Beware take care though no green-eyed dragon
With or without a baker's dozen of tails appeared
Not even a leafy sea dragon
Fortunately the ever present rocks remained
In all their ancient weathered splendour
Sculpted and shaped
By countless southern gales and tides
Burnt by a myriad of sun-parched summer skies
Lying athwart the shell-strewn beach
Banded here and there by crystalled quartz

Striking evidence of Vulcan's hand
Even a robust anticline bristling with complexity
Inviting wonderment
Though our surfers may well prevail
Seemingly secure in choosing
An easier way of life

Ars Longa Vita Brevis

Wandering free under café tables
A lone pigeon pretending to be a sparrow
Searching for crumbs
Dodging the feet of clod-hopping tourists
And the stiletto heels
Of the uniformly black-clad
Young office women all envious
Of their older clones already knocking
On the glass ceiling of promotion
A similar parade of peacock-proud
Male counterparts close by
Even mingling opportunistically
Some already on the rise
To even greater heights
Wearing expensive Italian models
Custom made with inbuilt lifts
Adding to their wearers' illusions
We elderly four seated securely protected
By the barrier of our combined ages
Enjoying good coffee
Blown as they say away
By the astonishing quality
Of the fabulous Year 12 exhibition
Upstairs gallery to the right
Each young artist displaying without exception
Sophisticated skills in their chosen medium
Well above we agree expected norms
Pooling our collective knowledge and imaginations
Art work leavened by loving ties
To friends and family close or extended

Fittingly completed with mature explanations
Of purpose and intent
No hollow mission statements here
Demonstrating beyond all reasoned doubt
That there may yet be hope
For a tortured world
Sadly in all of this
Our wandering identity confused sparrow
Elected to disappear

Kojunup Coffee, Anyone?

Spoiled rotten to date
All the way from Perth to Albany
We were well due even overdue
For a dose of crap coffee
Sure enough when Kojunup happened to be chosen
For that mid-morning stop
Our luck ran out like the south-west's water supply
A dog leg around the houses
Left no other apparent choice save the only bakery
We three took up station at a table
While Mick our intrepid kitty-holder
Braved the waiting throng of locals
Peppered with blow-ins (like we three)
Our hopes buoyed by the sight
Of a proper looking espresso machine
Lurking behind shelves stacked with iced-up confections
Mated with plastic shrouded not-so-hot buns
Reminder of Easter's immanent arrival
On the glass-filled street door a large cow bell
Sounded its toll all but muted
By the shattering bang each time
An entering or exiting customer failed
To notice the absence of any device
To slow the door's speeding trajectory
Joining in then overshadowing the background bedlam
Came a rough old local yokel
Bellowing like a buffalo on heat
A stream of rapid fire unintelligible words
Directed at his stolidly unmoving wife
No doubt long inured to his tirades

I on the other hand sat much too close for comfort
And groaned aloud as the fusillade reached a crescendo
Fortune chose that moment (as I poised for flight)
To briefly smile when liquid landed awash
In saucers not so deftly handed
By a kitchen maid with coldly buttered Easter buns
Now plastic free but sadly stale from yesterday
Products worthy of a steadfast pilgrim's feast
Baring their Christian crosses
Against our unbelievers' pampered taste buds
We sighed collectively our thoughts as one
Then with awareness of disaster about to strike
Each raised a cup and tentatively sipped
In unison four pairs of eyes looked heavenwards
At the fly-blown ceiling in disbelief
No barista's hand had played a part
In their contents brewing
Our morning coffee jaunt in this rural place
Easily fulfilled our worst predictions
We all agreed while hastening to depart
Trying graciously to accept defeat
And praying that tomorrow's caffeine delivery
Would once more restore the balance of our score

19 September 2001

Driving north through the dead
Of the afternoon
A trio of magpies
Darted across our path
Like miniature fighter planes
On a strafing run
Triggering for me
Replays of the crumbling
Disintegrating twin towers
And flashbacks
To the scything
Dying jet liners
Imshi Allah! America
Welcome to the real world
You have created

On Wrens

Fairy wrens
Are such beautiful little birds
Even Jenny
In her dowdy housekeeper's uniform
Is delightfully fetching
As she bustles around
Busily harvesting
For her youngster
And her faithful knight
In his brilliant blue suit
Of armorial splendour
A tiny white blaze
At his throat
Like a lady's dainty ribbon
Worn gallantly into battle
By her chosen champion
But briefly
On this autumn morn
No rival appears
To disturb the tranquillity
Of the moment
Even a plump New Holland honeyeater
Homing in
On an inviting spray of scarlet bottle brush
Elicits no response
(Thus demonstrating the possibility of peaceful
coexistence – assuming anyone out there is even
slightly interested)

Hear the Pennies Dropping

How immensely sobering this final act
The far horizon dotted with the debris
Of earlier warnings mainly unheeded
Perversely in the absence of rockets'
Red glare now the realisation has dawned
Something heavier than a penny has indeed
Dropped welcome to old age as quite suddenly
Actuarial tables have caught the body unawares
With no relief likely instead the long-banished
Fear of death chooses to return overshadowing
All other considerations and this time Mafeking
Will not be relieved

And Finally

Through all the long years
I've always taken care
To have a fallback position
Or so I thought
What a nonsense
What a stupid conceit
I now realise
There is only one reality
Only one positive
Forget taxes
Death is our destiny
Our sobering reward
For the miracle of life

The Suicide

Chris tied the rope
Around the roof truss
In his shed
Formed a noose
Slipped it over his head
Crying wet tears
Down glistening cheeks
Rivulets in black stubble
On his still baby face
A once-sweet much-loved kid
Crying out for help
Stupid drunken unworthy bitch
Not listening not caring
All this while he's perched
On the handyman's friend
Common or garden
Aluminium stepladder
Not famous for stability
Now to be suicides
Silent ally: Chris
Manages to maintain
A semblance of balance
While extracting today's
Essential life support tool
From the pocket
Of his jeans
Flicks the tiny screen
Until its bursts with light
Strokes the bitch slut's
Well remembered number

Already half-pissed
She mumbles in answer
To his despairing call
Cry in the wilderness
Listen to me for Christ's sake
I'm standing on a ladder
In the shed rope tied to a truss
Noose around my neck
Get in your fucking car
And get here quick
Five minutes
Or I'll kick the ladder away
Sobbing fucking rotten drunken bitch
But I love her can't stop
God! How it hurts
Slut on the other end
Croaks through the snot
Through the quick hot tears
Tries to brush away the booze
Flicks her screen
His mate's number
I dunno what to do
She snivels down the phone
Ring the cops now
You stupid fucking cunt
Quick! Quick!
Chris stows his phone
Still crying sobbing moaning
Delirious in his pain
Fate just then decides to intervene

His dumb mutt of a dog
Tired of playing alone
Wags in through the partly open door
Loves his alpha male to bits
On meaty hairy paws
Bounds across the slippery concrete floor
All enthusiasm puppy wants to play
Fuck off sobs Chris get out
Get out you stupid bitch go
Go now he tries to roar
Thus encouraged the mongrel mutt
Has another go and charges
Into one slim aluminium side
The flimsy hinge decides to fold
Five minutes a quick response
Two young cops flinch
But swiftly cut Chris down
Loosen the nylon noose
Apply CPR the kiss of life
Then the ambos the siren ride
On life support for days
In vain we who knew him
Share in the grief

Tripping Down the Garden Path

Somehow an ignominious defeat became
So we are told
The apotheosis of this nation
A huge continent
Sparsely populated
Lost a yet to flower generation
Presumably their best
Yet to come
Amongst the many boys from the bush
Doctors scientists engineers thinkers
Writers poets teachers philosophers
Collective nation building promise
Destroyed like so many rabbits
In the spotlight's beam
For what pray?
To satisfy emperors at play
Cousins matching cousins
With dreadnoughts not Dinky toys
Inbred and interbred
Funny money easily found
For big boys toys
No social progress in poison gas
Caterpillar-treaded tanks
Or *flammenwurfer*s thanks
Just an old familiar refrain
Tripping down the crazy
Garden path of history
All we like sheep following
Our bellwether leaders
To the promised land of hard knocks
Where not opportunity but spin doctors
Now hold sway

Spellbound

Spellbound in the great Tingle forest
Listening to the quietness
This in spite of other waves
Of many fellow travellers
Of many fellow tourists
With noisy small children
At their beck and call
The seemingly eternal giants
Mute and aloof
Absorbing every sound
Every repeated platitude
Like nowhere else
I've ever been

Meditation On Dishwashing

My second wife – whose mother
Was of Lebanese extraction
Taught me – as she had been taught
Not that their menfolk were ever initiated
In this arcane art – the correct way
The approved sequence in which
To carry out the great clean-up
In the aftermath of a meal – the breaking
Of far more than just bread
Invited early on in our brief marriage
Before the great disillusion broke over me
To an extended family occasion
I effectively and unthinkingly blotted
My male copybook postprandial
And anxious to please both wife
And formidable mother-in-law
By joining them and other wives
Sisters girlfriends aunts and grandmothers
In the large kitchen and picking up
A tea towel any mutual interest
In me or my well-being vanished
As the male brethren without exception
Looked at me with expressions of pain
Horror and or sorrow on their dark visages
I quickly beat an ignominious retreat
Out into the extensive grounds
Where my wife shortly joined me
In order to light up another of her
Inexhaustible supply of cigarettes
I was almost tempted to ask for one
But there's a limit to everything

On Not Listening

Have you noticed perchance
How nobody listens to what you have to say?
In point of fact – going further, seems to me
No one ever listens to anyone else
Unless the voice is emanating
From the possessor's iPhone
iPad or whatever happens to be
The latest flavour of the month
Flavour of the minute technological
Triumph: tried ordering a cup
Of weak black tea or a flat white
With a double shot lately
In any favoured franchise?
Without exception tea bag nestling
In its cup or a brace of its clones
Stewing in the pot – the one with
The obligatory flash-flooding spout
Will arrive accompanied by a small jug
Of milk and if you happened to specify
No sugar thanks dear, two paper cylinders
Of sweetness will be lying in the saucer
With a touch of bilge water of course
Or as you nominate a double shot
With the dragon at the cash register
And wait expectantly plastic in hand
She shifts her wad of gum to the other
Cheek and says while looking elsewhere
'Did yers want a double shot?'
Instead of a flat white a cappuccino
Sometimes appears at one's elbow

Oh well, close I suppose or as a sick friend's
Husband found after carefully detailing
Cold milk in a glass with a squirt of coffee
On the side was delivered of a tall glass
Brim full of ice stained from within
What more would one expect
In this happy land where franchises breed
Faster than any where else in the known world

The Politics of Envy

I clocked the new sleek Aston Martin
Out of the corner of my jaundiced eye
As I stepped off with the other sheep
On the greenman's long awaited appearance
Then as it burbled across the city intersection
With the flow the rear number plate stood out
E N V ME
Jesus wept! What is it with people today?
Bad enough the run of the mill offerings
You know MUM 64 or WIFEY 59
Drongos wasting their money giving yet more
To an always greedy government – stupid
The Aston's smart-arse driver young
Business executive type looked hardly old enough
To have earned the down payment
More likely a gift from dad and mumsie
Reward for good behaviour perhaps
What will his next pressie be I wonder
When he gets the hyphenated girlfriend
In the duff or gets caught sniffing coke
Cock embedded in a bit of rough
No mate I'm not envious in the least
He's welcome to his lot although
A tasty vintage or classic model
Fully restored in British racing green
Might just find me tempted
With a proper number plate of course

That's Life

Even the pines dotting this landscape
Far from their own island home
Seem apprehensive this morning
As well they might given the forecast
Forty degrees down here at the seaside
A roasting forty-two in town catastrophic
Fire danger in the hills and elsewhere
The black sentinel crows caark a portent
As I walk beneath: their dying notes
Resound like a soothsayer's prediction
Sending a shiver down my sweating spine
Momentarily cold in spite of the heat
Already shimmering up from the melting
Bitumen roadway as the dragon's breath
From the north from the baking inland
Licks out an early warning
The sea looks like molten glass
Dotted with board riders patiently waiting
To catch a wave but for now there is only
A restless swell on this the second day
Of another year yesterday we toasted
Its arrival as custom demanded
With dear friends the one already finishing
Her days in the certain knowledge
Of death's imminence her partner for more
Than half a century may soon go swiftly
Down the same path managed by the guardians
Of our health he however is undeterred
When told what the scan revealed
Simply laughed and in his best Bermondsey
Said, 'Well, that's life, in'it?'

At Petaluma

Water cascades
Ripples on steel
Light focuses
On the rotating wheel
Sunlight glistens
On rivulets forming
Then dissolving
On the deck
We pose
With our glasses
Our goblets of wine
Held aloft
Toasting our cleverness

Jaqui Hicks Retrospective

Cool grey greens
Dappled flanks interwoven
In a pattern of play
Bare-breasted Mona Lisa
With a proper smile
Look around
At a life's work
Gradations of change
Landscapes to love
And return to
Again and yet again

The Lily Pond

In the lily pond
The grey heron
Takes a yabby
Struts off
Tossing the ill-fated crustacean
In the air
Dropping then skilfully
Re-catching it
In the process of dismemberment
For which its slender bill
Seems ill-suited
In the lily pond
I look without success
For another yabby
Finding instead
An empty coke can
A light globe
And a part submerged
Upside down Nike trainer
The water is evil-looking
But still sustains
Assorted insects
And other forms of life
From the surrounding bushes
The many dead leaves droop
Wilt and eventually fall
Adding their flavour
To the uninviting brew

No Problem

Have you happened to notice
How young people
Stuck in the seven-day
Part-time servile service
Industries of growth
So beloved of politicians
Theorists and statisticians
In general are not amused
By our aged attempts
At levity only their own kind
It seems can penetrate
That carefully cultivated
Carapace of ennui
Which shrouds both genders
In our wearisome presence
But if by chance
A point of commonality
Is found a chink may appear
Even a fleeting smile
After the inevitable utterance
Of 'No problem'
Although I must confess to be
At a loss to understand
Why the simple request
For a long black for example
Should present a problem
To a presumably educated
And hopefully intelligent
Young person trained to operate
Those steamy glittering
Oh so sophisticated coffee machines!

My Friend the Recluse

Dear Bron is becoming even more of a recluse
These days heading rapidly towards
Three score years and ten living alone
The mainly lonely years since her divorce
Pretty well fixed now in her ways
But still devouring much factual writing
No ladies' book club choice or Mills and Boon
Rubbish litters her shelves we differ over
The *Weekend Oz* I won't tolerate Murdoch's
Anointed scribblers but she even finds pearls
Of wisdom where they vent their right wing
Spleen and says, 'I have to know what they
Are thinking so I can analyse.' No, sorry luv
Let's beg to bicker and move on
Sadly she no longer has the urge to paint
Her wondrous surreal landscapes of the past
Hopefully just a passing phase
Instead finds inspiration in her vegie patch
Growing enormous capsicums and much more
Tells me a simple cautionary tale of fright
On finding a swarm of bees settled
Across her compost pile (we share an allergic
Reaction to their stings) but unthinking for once
And quite annoyed she waved her arms
To shoo them off luckily for once no defensive
Squadron rose up to fight then later came the rain
She chanced to find a waterfall drowning
Ever willing workers by the score
Realising they posed no threat and impressed now
By their devotion to the common good she rescued

Many from their watery fate with arthritic fingers
Plucking them up by bedraggled wings
Then setting them out to dry not to rot
In the shelter of her potting shed
A triumph then of practicality and more
An appreciation of the bee and their devotion
To each other and community as Bron says
'Pity we aren't more like bees.' How could I not
Find myself nodding thoughtfully in agreement?

Happy Shopping

Under sufferance
I was shuffling along
Behind herself in Cheap as Chips
Or some such emporium
Catering to the great Oz underclass
Set up solely to prise hard-won dollars
From their pockets and purses
To pay for the ever-burgeoning imports
From Mao's transformed land
Everything from nail polish to disposable nappies
And worse
I'd been instructed to look out for preserving jars
Since something had gone wrong
Somewhere in the great unknown
Scheme of things or maybe
It was down to global warming
Anyway we had a kitchen and laundry
Overflowing with ripe apricots
Last year the bloody tree was bare
Seriously weird
We both spotted the elusive jars at the same time
And skidded to a halt
Done up in boxes of three
With proper screw on lids beauty bottler
And only six dollars a pop wacko!
Just then as we headed
For the only personed check-out register
(We can't have staff and cheap prices!)
Came an incredible scream
High-pitched and then sustained

Obviously a small child
Sounding in considerable distress
We wove our way through the throng
Standing slack-jawed before hardening
Into the inevitable queue
Like the well-trained Shoppers they all were
Past the checker-outer chick came two
Largish WASP self-important males
Clad alike in token uniforms of white
With assorted insignia proclaiming security
Phone pouches attached to wide black belts
Around their ample waists
Meantime the screaming
Had continued unabated
To be revealed as emanating
Out of a small infant
Struggling to emerge from a tattered pusher
Wheeled by an equally down-at-heel woman
For the moment held in check
By an ample blonde
Clad in navy blue shirt and slacks
Clearly a safe-guarding store person
The security detail homed in
And it became clear
That the hapless creature with the screaming kid
Had attempted to knock off some object of appeal
From the cornucopia of groaning shelves
And hide it in the pusher
Inevitably to be to be spotted
By the lynx-eyed dragon on her TV monitor

Luckily we were able to jump a few places
As the spectacle unfolded
Paid for our precious jars
And hastily exited through the sliding doors
The scream still reverberating in my aching head
On the descending escalator
I found myself wondering why
How hard up would you have to be?
And how ignominious
To be knocked off for shoplifting
In such a place when there are at least
Two perfectly acceptable
Jewellers I noticed down the road
Just begging to be robbed
One on the ground floor quite close by
The other even bigger sitting waiting
Near the booze shop
Surely just a piece of cake?
No thanks not me mate
Coming dear

Post Orstraya Day

Our beach was well nigh deserted
This morning just now save for the few
Hardy souls like me braving July in
January most of the lately holiday making
Workforce has scurried off back to town
Just like the marauding ants that disappeared
Overnight from our pantry once the honey
Laced with Ant-Rid began to bite
Poor nine to fivers the Damoclean job threat
Now sounded its warning knell and off they went
In their legions of mainly monstrous SUVs
Pack racks jammed full like Santa's cave
With all the paraphernalia lately required
To make the long days complete bicycles
Tricycles boogie boards beach balls and more
Yesterday in our local store braving brawny surfers
And their buxom blonde wenches all tatts
And brief T-shirts emblazoned with phrases
From which dear old auntie May would have
Averted her gaze while making the signs of the
Catholic cross it was like fighting a pathway
Through Johnie's after-Christmas sales
You may have noticed too that even the kids
Are growing bigger when I finally made it
To Kathie's crowded counter with my litre
Of milk we exchanged glances as she rang up the till
But said nothing just shrugged our shoulders
And briefly smiled no need for words maybe she
Snatched a sleep-in today money after all
Is far from being everything

Dayo, Dayo

Inexorably the days follow each other
Already its Monday again not that it matters
Surely once retired the divisions are meaningless
The hard part is getting up of a morning
Now it's Tuesday again and hang on
That means bin day my job my task
What did I put out last week one or two?
Need to have a wander and check out
The street over the road's blue bin's
Been sitting on the footpath for days
No help there 'course they do drive
A black BMW SUV when they come
Down to enjoy their holiday home
The negatively geared investment property
Take a squint further afield Ah! Yes!
A couple of yellow bins up the hill
Now I know we'll get woken in the morning
Some ungodly hour two fucking great trucks
About all we get for paying our rates
Must have slept through the din its Wednesday
My turn to dream up something for tea
Or dinner if you prefer looks like pasta
To me bit of onion bit of garlic some pesto
Tin of those little Italian cherry tomatoes
Easy look its bedtime again Christ!
Squint at the clock daylight Thursday
Blood test down the street early for me that is
Hello love! Yes good to see you too Rosie
Try the left arm today bit of a bloody pincushion
The other one thanks for that bye now the chemist

Sorry! Pharmacist and a bit of shopping done
Now Friday's with us what's to do better wash
The car strewth that's hard work bit hot today
Need a sit down and a glass of water thanks darl.
Looks better when it's washed doesn't it?
P'raps you might vacuum the inside darl
When you get a minute bloody hell!
Have to be at Centennial Park by one
Fred's funeral why anyone would want to be
Buried here with all those strangers is beyond me
Tea and bikkies of course rather have a glass

Of red in a pub so would Fred I'm certain
Specially at this his final bloody curtain
Bet his missus had her usual way hello Marg!
Ouch! Don't poke me so hard darl I'm awake
Thought we'd have a bit of a lie in since
It's Saturday oh all right what's her face's
Coming for lunch shit! She's another whingeing
Old bitch not out loud I hasten to add well
Sunday's another matter definitely time for that
Lovely long rest – actually I've been thinking darl
Yea I know – just listen – when I drop off the perch
Tell you what I'd like get Charlie to give
You a hand drop me in the old tinnie and
Run it down to the beach start up the Pelican
You remember how then slosh us all over with
The spare can of fuel push out a way next bit's
Tricky while you jam the throttle open have Charlie
Flick a match both of you stand well back

As me and the tinnie zoom out to sea
What a great way to go! I always thought
There's a touch of the old Viking in me
Somewhere come on darl say yes there's a pet

www.ingramcontent.com/pod-product-compliance
Lightning Source LLC
Chambersburg PA
CBHW070918080526
44589CB00013B/1347